National Costumes of the Old World

by

Ann Holmes

Chelsea House Publishers

CHELSEA HOUSE PUBLISHERS

Editor-in-Chief Stephen Reginald
Managing Editor James D. Gallagher
Production Manager Pamela Loos
Art Director Sara Davis
Picture Editor Judy Hasday
Senior Production Editor Lisa Chippendale
Designers Takeshi Takahashi, Keith Trego

First Printing

1 3 5 7 9 8 6 4 2

Library of Congress Cataloging-in-Publication Data

Holmes, Ann (Ann E.)
National costumes of the Old World / by Ann Holmes.

   p. cm. — (Looking into the past)
Includes bibliographical references and index.
Summary: Describes traditional costumes from around the
world, with a focus on Europe.

ISBN 0-7910-4684-2

1. Costume—Cross-cultural studies—Juvenile literature.
[1. Costume.]   I. Title.   II. Series.
GT518.H65   1997   97-27223
391'.0094—dc21   CIP
                                            AC

CONTENTS

CULTURE, CUSTOMS, AND RITUALS

The important moments of our lives—from birth through puberty, aging, and death—are made more meaningful by culture, customs, and rituals. But what is culture? The word *culture,* broadly defined, includes the way of life of an entire society. This encompasses customs, rituals, codes of manners, dress, languages, norms of behavior, and systems of beliefs. Individuals are both acted on by and react to a culture—and so generate new cultural forms and customs.

What is custom? Custom refers to accepted social practices that separate one cultural group from another. Every culture contains basic customs, often known as rites of transition or passage. These rites, or ceremonies, occur at different stages of life, from birth to death, and are sometimes religious in nature. In all cultures of the world today, a new baby is greeted and welcomed into its family through ceremony. Some ceremonies, such as the bar mitzvah, a religious initiation for teenage Jewish boys, mark the transition from childhood to adulthood. Marriage also is usually celebrated by a ritual of some sort. Death is another rite of transition. All known cultures contain beliefs about life after death, and all observe funeral rites and mourning customs.

What is a ritual? What is a rite? These terms are used interchangeably to describe a ceremony associated with a custom. The English ritual of shaking hands in greeting, for example, has become part of that culture. The washing of one's hands could be considered a ritual which helps a person achieve an accepted level of cleanliness—a requirement of the cultural beliefs that person holds.

The books in this series, *Looking into the Past: People,*

Places, and Customs, explore many of the most interesting rituals of different cultures through time. For example, did you know that in the year A.D. 1075 William the Conqueror ordered that a "Couvre feu" bell be rung at sunset in each town and city of England, as a signal to put out all fires? Because homes were made of wood and had thatched roofs, the bell served as a precaution against house fires. Today, this custom is no longer observed as it was 900 years ago, but the modern word *curfew* derives from its practice.

Another ritual that dates from centuries long past is the Japanese Samurai Festival. This colorful celebration commemorates the feats of the ancient samurai warriors who ruled the country hundreds of years ago. Japanese citizens dress in costumes, and direct descendants of warriors wear samurai swords during the festival. The making of these swords actually is a separate religious rite in itself.

Different cultures develop different customs. For example, people of different nations have developed various interesting ways to greet each other. In China 100 years ago, the ordinary salutation was a ceremonious, but not deep, bow, with the greeting "Kin t'ien ni hao ma?" (Are you well today?). During the same era, citizens of the Indian Ocean island nation Ceylon (now called Sri Lanka) greeted each other by placing their palms together with the fingers extended. When greeting a person of higher social rank, the hands were held in front of the forehead and the head was inclined.

Some symbols and rituals rooted in ancient beliefs are common to several cultures. For example, in China, Japan, and many of the countries of the East, a tortoise is a symbol of protection from black magic, while fish have represented fertility, new life, and prosperity since the beginnings of human civilization. Other ancient fertility symbols have been incorporated into religions we still practice today, and so these ancient beliefs remain a part of our civilization. A more recent belief, the legend of Santa Claus, is the story of a kind benefactor who brings gifts to the good children of the world. This story appears in the lore of nearly every nation. Each country developed its own variation on the legend and each celebrates Santa's arrival in a different way.

New rituals are being created all the time. On April 21, 1997, for example, the cremated remains of 24 people were launched into orbit around Earth on a Pegasus rocket. Included among the group whose ashes now head toward their "final frontier" are Gene Roddenberry, creator of the television series *Star Trek,* and Timothy Leary, a countercultural icon of the 1960s. Each person's remains were placed in a separate aluminum capsule engraved with the person's name and a commemorative phrase. The remains will orbit the Earth every 90 minutes for two to ten years. When the rocket does re-enter Earth's atmosphere, it will burn up with a great burst of light. This first-time ritual could become an accepted rite of passage, a custom in our culture that would supplant the current ceremonies marking the transition between life and death.

Curiosity about different customs, rites, and rituals dates back to the mercantile Greeks of classical times. Herodotus (484–425 B.C.), known as the "Father of History," described Egyptian culture. The Roman historian Tacitus (A.D. 55–117) similarly wrote a lengthy account about the customs of the "modern" European barbarians. From the Greeks to Marco Polo, from Columbus to the Pacific voyages of Captain James Cook, cultural differences have fascinated the literate world. The books in the *Looking into the Past* series collect the most interesting customs from many cultures of the past and explain their origins, meanings, and relationship to the present day.

In the future, space travel may very well provide the impetus for new cultures, customs, and rituals, which will in turn enthrall and interest the peoples of future millennia.

Fred L. Israel
The City College of the City University of New York

CONTRIBUTORS

Senior Consulting Editor FRED L. ISRAEL is an award-winning historian. He received the Scribe's Award from the American Bar Association for his work on the Chelsea House series *The Justices of the United States Supreme Court*. A specialist in early American history, he was general editor for Chelsea's *1897 Sears Roebuck Catalog*. Dr. Israel has also worked in association with Dr. Arthur M. Schlesinger, jr. on many projects, including *The History of U.S. Presidential Elections* and *The History of U.S. Political Parties*. They are currently working together on the Chelsea House series *The World 100 Years Ago,* which looks at the traditions, customs, and cultures of many nations at the turn of the century.

ANN HOLMES has been writing professionally for over 15 years, and is also editor of a literary journal, *The Loyalhanna Review*. She first became aware of traditional costume as a foreign exchange student to Thailand. Mrs. Holmes, her husband, and two children live in Pennsylvania.

OVERVIEW
Traditional Old World Costumes

From the time when early people first used crude animal skins to protect their bodies, clothing has been, along with food and shelter, necessary for supporting life. But clothing plays a much more important and complex cultural role in human life than simply providing protection from the elements. Styles of clothing are influenced by many different and often unexpected factors beside what is merely "fashionable." Clothing is greatly influenced by climate and cultural traditions, and can identify the wearer's geographic area, marital status, job, religion, social status, or political beliefs.

For example, in traditionally conservative Islamic countries, religious beliefs dictate that women outside of the home be robed and heavily veiled to shield them from the stares of unfamiliar men. In Western countries, a dark tailored suit is considered appropriate business attire for both men and women, while health professionals often wear distinctive white uniforms. Even in late 20th century American society, urban street gangs often use specific clothing or jewelry styles to identify members of their group.

Costumes of different world cultures may seem unusual or exotic, but they reflect both the climate and traditions of their people. Likewise, many similarities in the costumes can be traced to cultural exchanges, through exploration or conquest, between diverse ethnic groups. Although Western clothing is now commonly worn around the world (denim blue jeans are a perfect example), traditional apparel still plays an important role in maintaining the heritage of different peoples. Traditional clothing provides links to the past, and fascinating insights into the people, places, and customs of the world.

BAVARIA

B avaria, the largest state in Germany, is located in the extreme southeast of the country. It is a mountainous, forested area dominated by the Bavarian Alps. A picturesque region, Bavaria is an important tourist destination in Germany.

Traditional Bavarian women's costume generally uses brighter colors than those of the northern regions of the country. This skirt, which here is worn shorter than the more usual mid-calf length, is full and covered by a darker contrasting apron. Skirts are often boldly trimmed, with the aprons edged in needlework. A white blouse is worn over a black velvet bodice. The dirndl, or bodice is worn with a low neckline, and is laced by silver chains held by silver buttons. The front of the bodice is traditionally garnished with a small bouquet of fresh flowers. This Bavarian woman also wears a long-fringed, light silk shawl embroidered with a flower pattern in pastel shades. The shawl is worn over the shoulders, with the ends tucked into the bodice.

Traditional German women's costumes feature an extensive array of headdresses, depending on the region and social status of the wearer. These range from an embroidered fabric tiara-style cap to large black bows with streaming ribbons, and from white bonnets to simple kerchiefs and straw hats with large pompoms. The girl shown here wears a typical Alpine-style hat, generally made of wool or felt and trimmed with cording, a feather cockade, and ribbons in the back. She wears a flat, pointed shoe, here in a sling-back style, with white stockings.

BULGARIA

A Balkan country bordering the Black Sea in central Europe, Bulgaria is a center of Slavic culture. Because of its position along trade routes, Bulgaria was greatly influenced by Byzantine, Greek, Russian, and western civilizations throughout its history.

This costume is typical of that worn by both single and married women until the 19th century. The dress is of raw white silk, vividly decorated with bold horizontal bands of braid and needlework on the bodice, hem, and sleeves. The dress is topped with both an overskirt and an apron of wool felt. With the exception of weddings and other special occasions, a simple kerchief is worn on the head.

Just as additional layers of clothing are added as the weather cools, footwear changes seasonally. The sandals shown here are made of pigskin, and worn without socks during the summer. In the colder winter months, Bulgarian women traditionally wore brightly colored socks with these leather sandal-like shoes.

An additional overdress of thicker material would also be added in the winter. A sheepskin coat, with the wool worn inside, and a woolen scarf, are worn during severe winter weather by both men and women, although men also wear a tall sheepskin hat without a brim, the *tarboosh*.

Bulgarian men have traditionally worn thick blue embroidered shirts, bright cummerbunds, and woven trousers, which are laced with garters from the knee to the ankle. Dress clothing for men often consisted of white trousers or breeches trimmed in black braid and worn with a short jacket.

COSSACKS

The Cossacks were peasant-soldiers in the Russian empire who held certain privileges in return for military service and were well known as daring horsemen. The Cossacks were generally from southern European Russia and adjacent parts of Asia, and their costumes reflect their native cultures.

The men shown here are wearing traditional Cossack costume from the Ukraine. The white linen shirt is embroidered with colorful bands, usually red and green, on the front and on the sleeve hems. A red triangular scarf, the *shlyk*, is knotted at the neck, and a fringed sash of red or green is worn over the tunic. A decorative flared coat of any length can also be worn on horseback.

The trousers are generally made of a dark, rough material and are worn baggy at the knee for ease on horseback. These breeches are tucked into high black boots. Slimmer-cut, legging-type trousers can also be worn, usually with bark shoes called *lapots*. A high wool or fur cap completes the outfit. Decorative daggers or swords are tucked into the belt. If guns are used, cartridge cases are crossed over the chest.

Cossack regiments wear this costume in black or darker colors for ordinary occasions and in white on parade.

Many Cossacks fought against the Red Army during the 1918–1920 Russian civil war. Although their communities were collectivized by the communists in the late 1920s, many of their traditions in music and dance survive. One of the Cossacks shown here is playing the national musical instrument of the Ukraine, the *bandura*.

CROATIA

O nce a part of Yugoslavia, Croatia is now an independent republic on the Balkan peninsula. The costumes shown here are from the traditionally agricultural township of Gospic, in the Lika district of the Dinaric Alps not too far from the Adriatic coast. As is common in many countries, the costume varies from province to province, and even from village to village within a province. These costumes are now most often worn on festive occasions or holidays.

Skirt lengths vary from area to area as well, and the skirt is worn short here, but the trim is still very traditional. The woman's white homespun skirt is trimmed in many different colors of braid and rickrack, and worn with a short white apron that has a double row of trim. Her blouse has long sleeves that are wide and self-fringed at the wrist, and are trimmed nearly to the elbow with embroidery. Her short, almost bolero-style vest is of a contrasting dark material, also trimmed with bright, thick braid. She is not wearing a headdress.

The man wears white, wide-legged trousers edged in braid at the ankles. The trousers are topped by a long-sleeved white tunic that ends in cuffs, and is caught at the waist by a wide sash-type belt. The skirt is embroidered on the placket, which is an opening in the skirt, and is worn here with a short, thickly trimmed vest made of a darker material, and small soft tie. His small round cap is sewn with a patriotic emblem.

GREECE (FESTIVE)

While Greek costume may bring to mind the draped tunic styles of ancient and classical Greece that had such a strong influence on the clothing of other civilizations, the country's traditional clothing has changed a great deal through the centuries. Greek clothing today clearly shows the influence of both the Byzantine Empire of the 15th century and Greece's Turkish and Balkan neighbors.

The costumes shown here were traditionally worn by the sons of wealthy families for weddings and other special occasions. The outfits are very similar to those of the Evzones, Greek light infantry soldiers who wear the famous white kilts called *fustanello*. These are full, billowed skirts made of cotton or linen that fall to the knee. The fustanello are worn with white woolen stockings or leggings tied with decorative tasseled garters, and leather shoes topped with pompoms of contrasting colors.

The matching shirts have full sleeves and are topped with an ornately corded and embroidered vest or tunic. Brightly colored sashes are tied around the waist. A cloth Phrygian cap that ends in a long tassel completes the outfit. With Greece's bright, clear sunlight, vivid reds and blues are used to provide striking contrast to the mostly white outfits seen here.

Greek influence on the clothing of western cultures is fascinating. Some 2,000 years ago, a Greek warrior traveled to one of the farthest outposts of the then-known world, the remote highlands of Scotland. The fustanello there evolved into the garment now recognized as the Scottish kilt.

GREECE (EVERYDAY)

Although a small country, Greece has a diverse topography and climate, ranging from dry, sunny plains to cold mountain ranges to warm coastal areas. Agriculture is a principal occupation in Greece, even though less than one-quarter of the land is arable. Also, although Greece is a Mediterranean country famous for its warm sunshine, the winter climate can be severe in the mountainous northern regions.

The boy shown here wears an outfit adapted for everyday wear in the northern Greek climate, where a rural farm or village life is common. This outfit is still quite similar to those of the *Evzones*, Greek light infantry soldiers, and those seen in the previous page, but there are some noticeable differences in the details. The main feature is still the knee-length linen or cotton *fustanello*, or kilt. Although the fustanello is worn with white woolen stockings or leggings, the garters are plain white, and not tasseled. The leather shoes are sturdy but plain, and there is no decorative sash.

The white shirt has long sleeves that are less full, warmer and more practical for daily life in a cooler climate. The tunic is much less ornately embroidered, and has developed an open sleeve that still covers and protects the arms. The cloth Phrygian cap is made of darker material, but retains the tassel.

Along Greece's coastal regions and on its islands, dark baggy trousers and a distinctive flat peaked cap are worn by men in favor of the fustanello. In many regions, Western clothing is worn.

GREECE (GIRLS)

These girls are wearing traditional costumes from three regions of mainland Greece: (from left) Thessalia, Macedonia, and Peloponnesus.

Despite regional differences in the clothing, there are a number of similarities. All three costumes feature mid-calf to ankle-length full skirts with decorative trim. Although different in design, the tops of these three costumes feature wide sleeves that don't quite reach the wrist. All three girls also wear distinctive headdresses.

Thessalia is on the central, fertile plain of Greece, and the Thessalian costume is somewhat similar to traditional Turkish clothing. In this costume, a length of sheer fabric falls from the mid-calf length skirt to the ankles, and the skirt itself is covered by a decorative small, distinctively pointed apron. The sleeves and neckline of the shirt are edged in lace. The small cap is also trimmed with embroidery.

Because Macedonia is located in the northern mountains of Greece, Macedonian attire reflects the strong Asian influence on the area. This girl wears a white linen blouse topped by a short, wide-sleeved overblouse trimmed in rickrack with bold, geometric design. Her white veil may be decorated in embroidery, and is trimmed with coins.

Clothing from the southern peninsula of Peloponnesus features the same full skirt now topped by a white blouse and a short bolero jacket. The trim of the jacket matches that of the skirt, and lace is again featured at the neckline and sleeves. The headpiece is flat, trimmed with dangling ribbons. A wide bracelet completes the ensemble.

HOLLAND

olland is another name for The Netherlands, a low-lying country of northwestern Europe on the North Sea. In Holland, as elsewhere, costumes differ from region to region and can indicate the wearer's religion.

The costumes shown here are from the village of Volendam, located in north Holland on the IJsselmeer, an inland body of water that was formed by damming the North Sea below the Frisian Islands. Because of the cool climate, layers of clothing are a feature of Dutch costume. The man's trousers are cut loose of dark woven material, probably in blue or black. He wears a lined cotton jacket of double-breasted cut that buttons high to the neck. Men in Volendam traditionally wore striped shirts with red collars and two filigree buttons. A scarf and dark fur cap complete the costume.

The woman wears a characteristic peaked lace bonnet, with side points. Her square cut bodice is filled with an embroidered kerchief worn over a layer of lightweight wool, and the sleeves reach the elbow. In Volendam, skirts traditionally had seven stripes of different colors, and were worn, as shown here, with a dark apron topped by a bright yoke. For special occasions, a number of petticoats are added to this basic costume, and a small frilled white apron is worn. Necklaces of garnets, carnelian, and coral were often worn in this area.

The distinctive wooden shoes commonly associated with outdoor wear in the Netherlands are not shown here. Flat leather slippers are generally worn at home.

HUNGARY

ocated in Central Europe, Hungary is bordered by Ukraine, Serbia, Slovakia, Romania, Croatia, Slovenia, and Austria. About 88 percent of the Hungarian people are Magyars, descended from the nomadic tribes who settled in the region. People of many other ethnic groups live in Hungary as well. Most of the land is a large fertile plain used for agriculture.

The girl's costume shows the ornate embroidery typical of the city of Kalocsa, in the southern central part of the country. She wears a white cotton skirt with a high-necked, short-sleeved blouse. Although the skirt is relatively simple, there is extensive embroidery and trim on the sleeves of the blouse and its overvest. A richly embroidered apron is worn over the skirt as well. The girl wears a simple kerchief wrapped around her head, and embroidered slippers with white stockings.

The boy's costume is from the Alfold, the great central plain of Hungary. He wears a *gatyak*—wide, loose pantaloons that resemble a divided skirt and that serve as protection from the summer sun. In some regions the gatyak is made of white wool bordered with a rough crocheted lace. Here, the gatyak and wide sleeved shirt are made of white linen and are fringed. The wide sleeves of the shirt can be partially sewn to make pockets.

A short, ornately braided vest is worn over the shirt. The boy also wears a small, round-brimmed, and high-crowned felt hat, and leather boots. A long, colorful coat would be added in the winter.

INDIA

The clothing of India is among the most colorful and striking in the world. Although India's distinctive caste system identifies its members by religion and social status, and there are many regional differences in costume, most women wear a draped garment of some kind.

The most important item of an Indian woman's wardrobe is the *sari*, pictured here. Saris are made of a single piece of fabric about six yards long and 40 or 45 inches wide. Saris are made of lightweight silk, cotton, or both, and feature intricate prints or embroidery. The saris of wealthy women are often embroidered with silver or gold thread.

A sari is worn over a short shirt or blouse and a long petticoat or slim trousers, depending on the religion or ethnic group of the wearer. It is folded into pleats around the waist to form a skirt, then brought up across the bodice and over the shoulder. The sari can also be draped over the head to form a veil.

The sari is extremely adaptable. Its loose drape and lightweight fabric protect the wearer from the intense heat, and it dries quickly during the rainy monsoon season. Originally a Hindu garment, the sari's length and modest drape is considered appropriate by women of many religious traditions. Subtle differences in folds can identify the wearer's religion.

Jewelry is an important accessory. Many women wear heavy and ornate earrings, necklaces, bracelets, armbands, rings, anklets, and nose studs every day. Flat leather sandals are usually worn with traditional clothing.

LATVIA (BARTA AREA)

atvia, formerly part of the U.S.S.R., is bordered by Estonia, Russia, Belarus, Lithuania, and the Baltic Sea. Its landscape features low plains dotted with forests, lakes, and streams. Temperatures can be extreme; winters are cold and snowy, and summers are hot. Lettish culture has been greatly influenced by that of Russia and the other ethnic groups who live there. Because flax is a major crop, linen is frequently used for clothing.

The costumes shown here are from the Barta district, near the Barta River, which empties into the Baltic Sea in southwest Latvia. The woman's soft, flat headdress indicates that she is married. She wears a long-sleeved white linen blouse with a band of trim from the shoulder to the elbow. The soft pointed collar and cuffs are both edged with needlework. Her long dark skirt is edged with several rows of bright and contrasting trim, as is the smaller matching vest. She wears a striking double strand of amber beads, for which Latvia is known.

The man wears a white costume decorated across the chest with colored bands and a double row of buttons. The stand-up collar is also trimmed. His tunic is belted with a broad woven sash whose pattern indicates the district in which he lives. The white pants fall into long cuffed breeches at mid-calf and are worn with white socks and leather shoes.

Today, these costumes are most often worn for ceremonial occasions.

LATVIA (RUCAVA AREA)

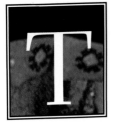

The Rucava area of Latvia is located along the shores of the Baltic Sea. Although Latvia is highly industrialized and has an agricultural tradition, its fishing industry is also very important.

While the costume of the man shown here is strikingly similar to that of the man from the Barta area of Latvia, there are subtle regional differences in the pattern of his woven belt and on the cuffs of his trousers. However, the pattern and cut of his long breeches-like trousers and decorated jacket are almost identical to those of his counterpart from Barta.

The women's costumes, however, vary a great deal. The woman shown here wears a high, brimless cap boldly decorated with shining patterns of beadwork and embroidery. Her dark, mid-calf length skirt features a single wide band of trim that is patterned with a stylized flower motif. Although her long-sleeved white blouse is also embroidered, the designs are strikingly different. Perhaps most unusual is her vest, which features dynamic colors and geometric trim. This vest also features a much higher neckline than the one from the Barta region. Her accessories also highlight the amber beading of Latvia.

This amber is a yellow or yellow-brown material found on the southern coast of the Baltic Sea. The brittle, fossilized resin of coniferous trees that are now extinct, amber comes in many shapes and is used often in the jewelry, artwork, and beadwork of the area. Occasionally, fossilized insects are found imbedded in the amber beads.

LATVIA (ABRENE AREA)

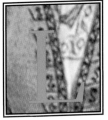

atvia's Abrene region is an inland district, with traditions, landscapes, and costumes quite different from those of the people living on the coast. The Abrene region is known for its streams, lakes, horses, and birch trees. These images are often seen in the traditional clothing of the region.

The man here is wearing a dark woven suit of trousers topped by a hip-length jacket of the same material, very different from the men's costumes seen previously. The trousers are worn tucked into socks at ankle length. The deep V-neck of the jacket is edged with trim in a distinctive scroll-work pattern, and braid trims the sleeves. The jacket is belted with a highly decorated, wide fringed sash, and worn over a soft-collared white shirt that is also embroidered along the placket and collar.

The woman's skirt and blouse are of a white woven fabric, contrasting with the Latvian costumes seen previously. The high-necked blouse has bands of embroidery running from the shoulder down and around the upper arm. The sleeves are quite full, then gathered into cuffs at the wrist. Her midcalf-length skirt is trimmed in wide bands at the bottom and with a narrow, simpler pattern at the waist. She is wearing two brooch-like pins just below the high collar of the blouse. Her white stockings are worn with flat, soft leather shoes.

The head covering is a small, round, brimless cap made of heavy fabric and covered with vivid needlework. This needlework contrasts with the overall simplicity of her costume.

LITHUANIA

Another of the former republics of the Soviet Union, Lithuania is located in northeastern Europe. It is bordered by Latvia, Russia, Poland, Belarus, and the Baltic Sea. Nearly 80 percent of its people are ethnic Lithuanians, and, because most Lithuanians are Roman Catholic, many of their ethnic traditions focus on this religion.

The cap-like headdress worn by these girls identifies them as unmarried; married Lithuanian women wear a kind of head scarf. These girls both wear full-sleeved white blouses with unique, heavily embroidered patterns on the collar and lower arm. Over the blouse, a distinctive, thickly patterned V-neck vest is worn, which ends in fringed bands on the girl on the left. Both vests are trimmed in horizontal designs and provide extra warmth in cool weather.

The skirts shown are both ankle length and made of a heavy, patterned material. The skirts are worn with a long apron in both costumes. Although colors are used quite differently in these aprons, the stylized flower motifs are very similar. A flat, rather pointed-toed shoe is worn.

With Lithuania also bordering the Baltic Sea, amber beads such as those worn in Latvia are quite popular here as well.

Because Lithuanian culture is tied so closely to its religion, many cultural customs were curtailed by a ban on religious practice during the period of Soviet rule, from 1940-1991. Since then, cultural traditions have been celebrated more openly, although traditional costume is still most often worn for special occasions.

NORWAY

(HARDANGER AREA)

n old Norwegian saying, "The sea unites us; the land divides us," helps explain many of the differences in regional dress in this country. Norway is narrow and rugged, with a coastline that runs about 1,700 miles. From here, fierce Norse sailors, the Vikings, colonized the islands from Scotland to Iceland and Greenland.

This costume is from the Hardanger area, in the southern part of Norway, and the layers of the outfit indicate the coolness of the climate. The full-sleeved white blouse is made of linen and worn with a colorful bodice and black skirt. The skirt is topped by a white linen apron with lavish openwork embroidery. Like the belt, the bodice is also heavily embroidered with both thread and beadwork. Vivid oranges and greens are used to contrast with the black pieces of the costume. Dark stockings and shoes complete the outfit.

Silver buttons, seen on the bodice here, are often used to decorate the traditional clothing of both men and women, and bridal crowns of silver are often used at Hardanger weddings.

Although this woman wears a small headdress trimmed with long ribbons, there are other distinctive headpieces of the Hardanger area. Young girls traditionally wore a square bonnet made of velvet or wool that was edged in velvet and trimmed with beading. Matrons wore the *skaut*, a large square of stiffly starched white linen that was folded, fastened in the back, and worn in a number of ways.

NORWAY
(SETESDAL AREA)

ike Hardanger, the Setesdal region of Norway has its own distinctive dress for both men and women because of the rugged terrain.

This black skirt is cut in a circular pattern, then stiffened and edged with broad bands of colored red and green material. The skirt is worn high over contrasting trimmed underskirts and a long-sleeved white linen blouse. The costume is worn with a very short, full-sleeved bolero jacket that is edged and trimmed with braid and closed with a silver clasp. The woolen sash, worn at the waist although the skirt rises higher, is fringed and usually knitted. A square-cut cap of dark material is also edged in braid. Flat black leather shoes that feature silver buckles are worn with dark stockings.

On festive occasions, the long-sleeved blouse is worn with a full, floor-length dress similar to a pinafore with an extremely high neckline. The shoulder straps and neckline are trimmed with a wide band in the red and green embroidery of the area, as is the hem. A small soft purse of black wool with stitchery and beadwork is carried.

Traditional clothing for men in the Setesdal region includes long black trousers thickly embroidered in reds and greens for about eight inches from the ankle to the knee. A black and white shirt with a white soft collar and intricate traditional pattern on the sleeves is worn under an ornately trimmed vest. Silver accents are used lavishly. The sleeve patterns are often seen in Norway's classic knit ski sweaters.

POLAND

ontact with a number of cultures has influenced traditional Polish costume, as has its variable climate. Poland is located in central Europe, bordered by the Baltic Sea, Russia, Lithuania, Belarus, Ukraine, the Czech Republic, Slovakia, and Germany. A major European power during the 15th and 16th centuries, Poland has been partitioned among Russia, Austria, Prussia, and Germany at various times in its history.

These costumes are from the Krakow region, the historical and cultural capital of Poland. They clearly show the use of stripes and bright color combinations, for which Polish costume is known, and would be worn for festive occasions.

The man's outfit features loose linen trousers with wide stripes tucked into soft leather boots that are mid-calf length. His long, vest-like jacket is collared but sleeveless, and is worn over a white linen shirt with a small collar and trimmed cuffs. The jacket is made of black wool and worn topped with a leather belt whose buckle is the Polish eagle. A tie and four-cornered hat trimmed with ribbon completes the costume.

The woman wears a bright cotton skirt trimmed with stripes of multi-colored embroidery. The apron is made of white lace and is exceptionally small. Her sleeveless and vividly trimmed bodice tops a white, elbow-length blouse of cotton or silk. Headdresses vary from region to region, but a scarf of some kind is often worn. Beads are a common accessory for Polish women, and shoes range from the flat pump seen here to high black boots.

POLAND (TATRA AREA)

he Tatra Mountains are the highest range of the Carpathian Mountains, located in southern Poland along its border with Slovakia. Sheep and cattle are herded along its high mountain pastures during the summer, and the area is known for its winter sports.

This boy's costume reflects the colder weather of his mountain region and is largely made of sheep's wool for warmth and durability. As in the rest of Poland, use of bright colors and embroidery are important. The light-colored trousers are worn to the ankles and have bold dark trim on the upper thighs. The boy's belt is a thick sash worn over the trousers, and the designs are similar on both.

A long-sleeved white shirt and soft, colored tie are worn underneath a sheepskin vest elaborately decorated with stylized flower motifs. This vest is worn with the warm fur turned in towards the body during the winter months, and outside in the summer. For extra protection from the weather, a short cape is worn. Worn at just below hip length, the cape is trimmed with geometric braid.

The soft woolen hat, with a small brim similar to those in other mountainous countries, is trimmed as well with a band of embroidery. Although these are not shown here, it is also common in the Carpathian Mountain regions to sew large and colorful pompoms onto coats.

Thick white socks are worn, and boots will most likely be substituted for the flat leather shoes shown here during the winter months. In earlier times, feet were bound with layers of cloth for protection from the weather.

SCOTLAND

The traditional dress of Scotland is well known and reflects a rich history.

The earliest tribes in northern Great Britain wore short pleated skirts, possibly adapted from contact with Greek explorers. With these first kilts, a rough shirt was worn, as was a woven woolen mantle of various colors, an early plaid. (Keep in mind that a plaid is the mantle, not the pattern of the material. The distinctive patterns of the material are the tartans.) Today's kilts are lengths of tartan material pleated to form skirts at or just above the knee.

Over time, tartans became identified with different clans. After Prince Charles Stewart ("Bonnie" Prince Charlie) failed in an attempt to unite the highland clans and wrest control of Scotland from the English in 1745, wearing tartans was outlawed until 1782.

This example shows full ceremonial dress of a Scottish regiment. A *sporran*, the fringed bag worn around the waist, helps anchor the kilt and serves as a purse. The kilts are worn with knee-length argyle socks, a small fringed garter, and black shoes, covered here by tall white spats.

The short tailored jacket is edged in heavy gold or silver braid. A tartan sash is draped from the shoulder across the chest to identify the wearer's clan or regiment. White gauntlets complete the man's uniform.

Scottish headgear comes in many styles. This man wears a military bearskin hat while the boy wears a *glengarry*, a straight, pointed cap edged in a red and white checked pattern with two streamers down the back. Also well known is the *tam-o-shanter*, a beret-style flat hat with a pompom on the top.

SILESIA

ilesia, a region of central Europe located primarily in southwest Poland and the northern Czech Republic, has been heavily influenced by German and Russian culture. Settled by Slavic peoples and contested by many neighboring states, Silesia was an important coal and manufacturing area. Silesia was divided between Germany, Poland, and Czechoslovakia after World War I, and areas of Silesia were repartitioned by Germany and Poland after World War II.

Traditional Silesian costume, such as shown here, is worn for special occasions only, and it shows the influence of many different cultures. This particular outfit shows a strong German influence, although the city of Cieszyn, where this costume originated, is in the Polish region, not far from the Czech Republic.

The white blouse is covered by a German-style sleeveless dirndl and worn with a full skirt. Although the short sleeves and narrow contrasting sash are often seen in Czech costume, traditional Silesian dress tends to have less lace trim and more conservative embroidery than Czech clothing.

As in Germany, headdresses are an important part of traditional Silesian costume. A starched, white crocheted lace cap is worn only by married women, and unmarried girls wear ribbons in their hair. Jewelry and beads are not worn with traditional Silesian attire.

Until fairly recently, men wore clothing identified with their trades. Miners and chimney sweeps both wore distinctive clothing that reflected Silesia's industrial heritage.

The Silesian region also lends its name to "silesia," a twilled cotton cloth produced there that is used primarily for linings and pockets.

SWEDEN

Throughout the countries of Scandinavia, the cool climate dictates that clothing be worn in layers to provide the most comfort and warmth possible.

In Sweden, almost every small village has its own traditional style of dress. In general, though, women's skirts are long, plain, and full. Stripes are an important design element, and the striped aprons worn indicate which region the wearer is from. Because Swedish women traditionally excelled in needlework such as knitting, lace, stitchery, and hemstitching, outfits are worn with heavily embroidered neckerchiefs, headgear, and other accessories.

The costumes shown are typical of the rural province of Dalarna, where traditional handicrafts, like ribbon weaving, are still practiced and costumes are worn for midsummer celebrations, weddings, and other festivities.

In Dalarna, women often wear a long-sleeved white blouse with a soft, turned-down collar. This is covered by an embroidered bodice that matches a small cap. Men typically wear a white shirt with a high collar, topped by a woven, waist-length blue jacket. Knee-length breeches made of sueded cotton are usually tan and worn with embroidered garters. Knit stocking caps are traditionally worn by men in this area.

As with other attire, headgear varies from region to region in Sweden. Women's caps may be small and embroidered, as shown here, or made of velvet, puffed linen, lace, or pointed muslin. Caps may be trimmed with ribbon or lace. Both men and women wear shoes with silver buckles, and women use silver earrings, pendants, necklaces, and belts.

UKRAINE
(LOWLANDS)

ow a republic in Eastern Europe, Ukraine was formerly the Ukrainian Soviet Socialist Republic of the Soviet Union (the U.S.S.R.). Since 1991, it has been the second largest country in Europe, after Russia.

A large portion of the country is flat, fertile plain, with the Carpathian Mountains looming in the west. The climate varies from sub-tropic on the Crimean Sea to more temperate on the plains and cooler in the mountains.

The costumes in this picture show everyday dress of agricultural Ukrainian peasants. The woman wears a wide-sleeved white blouse embellished with detailed embroidery along the length of the sleeves. Although the embroidery patterns vary from district to district, they are always very colorful, even more so for festive attire.

Her short, thickly pleated skirt is covered by a dark apron trimmed in braid of bold geometric design. The skirt just covers the tops of her high boots. Her waist-length head covering, traditionally trimmed with ribbons, is held in place by a floral band. She is holding a scythe, used for harvesting grain.

The man wears a long-sleeved white shirt trimmed in embroidery both at the wrists and along the placket, almost to the waist. His long, baggy trousers are tucked into low leather boots, and he wears a contrasting wide fringed sash at the waist. On his head, he wears the famous *shapka*, a tall, brimless hat made of curly ram's wool. The *shapka* may be dyed brown, gray, or black.

UKRAINE

(MOUNTAINS)

Although much of Ukraine is fertile plain, the Carpathian Mountains in the west, with their cooler climates at higher elevations, have a strong influence on the traditional clothing of the people there. Because Ukraine today is now highly industrialized and urbanized, traditional costume is generally worn for special occasions only.

The man shown here is wearing a traditional long-sleeved white shirt, heavily trimmed with vivid needlework around the short collar, along the placket, and around the cuffs. His short fur vest is richly decorated with appliqués of leather and beads, and he wears a wide woven sash at his waist. His loose trousers are worn as long breeches, and his flat, moccasin-like shoes lace up the leg over patterned socks. His hat has a low crown and flat brim, and greatly resembles that of the boy from the Tatra region of the Polish Carpathian mountains. He carries a walking stick that is topped by an ax-like handle.

The woman also wears a heavy fur vest, as ornately embroidered and appliquéd as the vest worn by the man. Her dark skirt is covered by a richly embroidered apron and reaches to just below the knee. As is common in Ukraine, her wide-sleeved white blouse is beautifully covered with embroidery from the shoulder to the wrist.

She also wears thick patterned socks with laced-up flat moccasins. Her head is covered by thick scarf for both modesty and protection from the weather. She is carrying a small, ornately decorated milk can.

YUGOSLAVIA
(WOMEN)

The former Yugoslavia was a melting pot of many different ethnic cultures, religions, and traditions, the combination of six republics: Serbia, Croatia, Slovenia, Montenegro, Bosnia-Herzogovina, and Macedonia (not to be confused with the area of Macedonia in Greece). Because of this ethnic diversity, there is no one costume that can be called typically "Yugoslavian." All are distinctive.

This woman wears a costume from the Posavina region of northern Croatia, a farming and fruit growing area. Although Croatian women wear skirts of varying lengths, depending on the region, this outfit is full length. The blouse is made of white linen and features a flat collar and very full sleeves. The bodice of the blouse is embroidered in vertical bands, and the sleeves are very ornately sewn in distinctive, intricate patterns, in a number of colors.

The full-length skirt is made of homespun white wool and covered with a long heavily embroidered felt apron. The embroidery patterns and colors identify the village of the wearer, and they may include special designs to ward off evil or encourage good luck. Soft flat leather shoes and embroidered socks, white for unmarried girls and blue for matrons, are also worn.

Although a headdress is not visible in this photograph, simple kerchiefs are most often worn. Another traditional form of headgear is a shoulder-length, or somewhat longer, white cloth worn with a tiny *kapa*, or hat. A sleeveless and collarless vest or jacket made of colored and embroidered felt is added when the weather becomes cool.

YUGOSLAVIA
(MEN)

s with women's clothing, the many different cultural and ethnic traditions of the former Yugoslavia are seen in a wide variety of clothing styles for the men of the area. In trouser styles alone, a number of variations are possible.

For example, in some Dalmatian and Serbian traditional costume, long trousers are worn rather baggy and loose, in a style influenced by Turkey. In some Montenegrin and Bosnian costume, these same Turkish-style trousers are worn as knee breeches. Another style features ankle-length trousers that are almost as slim as tights. Trousers are most often made of black, blue, or white fabric, again depending on the traditions of the region.

Whatever the tradition or style, though, embroidery is, as throughout the Balkan countries, an important aspect of costume for both men and women.

This costume identifies the man wearing it as being from the township of Vrlika in the region of Dalmatinska Zagora.

Men's clothing in this hilly region consists of five main pieces, with numerous variations in decoration: trousers, shirt, vest, sash, and belt. The long dark trousers are made of a rough-woven, homespun fabric. The intricately embroidered linen shirt is long, tunic length, with a soft collar and open placket emphasized with embroidery. The long sleeves end in wide cuffs.

A multicolored sash ending in a two- to three-inch fringe is worn over the shirt. A hip-length vest, collarless and sleeveless, is heavily covered with decorative needlework. The outfit is worn with hand-worked leather shoes.

CHRONOLOGY

30,000 years ago – Animal skins worn during the Ice Age in northern climates

3000 B.C. – Tunics and shawls worn in Sumeria

2000 B.C. – Egyptian men begin to wear basic tunics. Egyptian women wear close-fitting sheath gowns

600 B.C. – Greek men wear Ionic tunics; women wear draped garments

500 B.C. – Togas worn by Roman men; women wear tunics

600 B.C.–A.D.1100 – Early Western European dress develops

5th–11th centuries – Ornate clothing worn in Byzantine Empire

5th–14th centuries – Draped "medieval" clothing; headgear for men and women

14th–17th centuries – Rich clothing of the Renaissance period. Heavy brocades. Puritan influence seen in 17th century with more conservative clothing.

18th century – Pale colors and delicate materials more predominant. Skirts are wider, and hair begins to be powdered. Knee breeches remain common for men.

19th century   Classical Greek revival styles worn by women evolve into ornate Victorian bustles. Men's trousers lengthen to ankles

Early 1900s –   Women's fashions straighten, skirts remain at ankles

1920s –   Hemlines rise for women in "flapper" styles

Mid–1900s –   Conservative fashions during Depression and World War II. Slacks for women more accepted

1960s –   Miniskirts and "psychedelic" pop clothing. Synthetic fabrics more commonly used

1990s –   Office dressing becomes more casual. Styles change seasonally for men and women

INDEX ❀

FURTHER READING

Kindersley, Barnabas & Anabel. *Children Just Like Me.* New York: Dorling Kindersley, 1995.

Lister, Margot. *Costume: An Illustrated Survey from Ancient Times to the 20th Century.* Boston: Plays, Inc., 1968.

Mann, Kathleen. *Peasant Costume in Europe.* London: Adam and Charles Black, 1961.

Microsoft Encarta 96 Encyclopedia. Microsoft Corporation, 1995.

Microsoft Office Professional & Bookshelf. Microsoft Corporation, 1995.

Perl, Lila. *From Top Hats to Baseball Caps, From Bustles to Blue Jeans.* New York: Clarion Books, 1990.

Rowland-Warne, L. *Costume.* New York: Alfred A. Knopf, 1992.

Wilcox, R. Turner. *Folk and Festival Costume of the World.* New York: Charles Scribner's Sons, 1965.

World Book Encyclopedia. Chicago: Field Enterprises Educational Corporation, 1959.